Religious Studies
Series Editor: Davi[d]

GW01388330

Buddha: A Journey

David Naylor
Ann Smith

M

Macmillan Education

Contents

Foreword

In this book, we have tried to give you a picture of the Buddha's life, as well as describing and explaining his most important teachings. It has not been possible to tell you about all his ideas or of the various ways in which his followers have lived by them. Nevertheless, we hope that by the end of your journey through this book you will have found plenty of questions to ask about the Buddha, his work and ideas, and that you will be able to find out more information for yourself.

The life history of the Buddha is told in a way that you may not be familiar with. You may find some of the words difficult. Try to get the general idea of what is happening and ask your teacher for help if you need it. We have also used the proper words for the Buddha's ideas because in the language used by his followers they have a meaning that it is not always possible to translate into English.

There are many ways in which this book may be used. It may give you ideas for your own project work. You may use it as the main part of your course. The important thing to remember is that it is not a book of answers. There are always more questions to be asked and other kinds of information to be used.

In this book you will find that anything in

is a piece of factual information.

indicates an idea for you to think about or discuss.

Any blocks of type set in *italics* are stories told by the Buddha or about him.

Note Buddha refers to anyone who is an Enlightened Being. The Buddha refers to Siddhartha Gautama, who achieved enlightenment in the 5th century BCE. Both terms are used throughout the book.

Introduction

If you lived on the beautiful island of Sri Lanka and turned on the radio early in the morning you would hear a group of people chanting in a language called Pali:

I go to the Buddha for refuge.

I go to the Dharma for refuge.

I go to the Sangha for refuge.

Who is the Buddha? What do the words 'Dharma' and 'Sangha' mean?

This book will take you on a journey which will help you to find the answers to these and other questions. It will also try to help you to understand the journey that the Buddha made and how what he discovered still influences the way millions of people live today.

1

How do we know the Buddha existed?

The Buddha was a man. If you have never heard of him you may wonder how we have come to know about him. More importantly, you may wish to know why he should be part of your work in school. The first question we will try to answer now. The second question you may be able to answer for yourself at the end of the book.

Here is some information that may help you deal with the question of how we know that such a person existed.

We know that there once lived in India a man who was to become known as the *Buddha*. His original name was Siddhartha Gautama. How he became the Buddha will be described later on. The Buddha never wrote about himself and no one wrote about him whilst he was alive. Yet other men and women thought that the Buddha's ideas, teachings and discoveries were important enough to follow. One such man was the Emperor Asoka of India (274–236 BCE). It is not possible to be completely accurate, but a Ceylonese Chronicle says that Asoka reigned 218 years after the death of the Buddha. It was largely due to the fact that Asoka encouraged the followers of the Buddha that the Buddha's ideas and teachings spread through India.

After the Buddha's death at the age of 80, monks set about trying to remember all the Buddha had said. To do this the monks were divided into groups. Each group was given the job of remembering one particular part of the Buddha's teaching. When new people joined the groups, they were asked to learn the Buddha's teachings off by heart. In this way the Buddha's teachings were not only remembered but were spread to more and more people. We are not sure for how long this went on but some writers think it may have happened for at least 400 years.

About 250 BCE the Buddha's teachings were taken to the island of Sri Lanka. There the early Buddhist monks learned and passed on the teachings in an Indian language called *Pali*. They realised, however, that the teachings would have to be written down if they were not to disappear or be forgotten. In the first century BCE Sri Lanka suffered from a civil war and a famine, many monks died and at one time there was only one monk living who knew a certain part of Buddha's teachings. If he had died that teaching would have been lost forever! So the monks of Sri Lanka gathered together and wrote down all the sayings and teachings of Buddha. These writings became known as the *Pali Canon.*

Think spot

Have you noticed that we are using BCE and not simply BC? Can you find out why?

Read the piece of information again. Now look at the questions that follow. With a friend discuss what the answers might be. Now write your answers down.

Think spot

1 The information does not appear to have told us when the Buddha actually lived. Can you work out when he might have lived from the information given?

2 Why did the monks rely on their memories for so long? Why do you think they eventually wrote them down? What do you think they feared most?

3 Imagine that you live in a country where there is no paper, pens, computers and so on. Anything that is important has to be remembered. Instructions, laws, messages and stories about the past all have to be stored in peoples' memories.
   With your friend, work out ways in which you might help a young child grow up in such a country. Do you think that everyone should be expected to remember everything? Think about how the monks organised themselves.

4 Do you think that people should be encouraged to use their memories more? Give reasons for your answer.

2
The story begins

Who was the Buddha? The *Pali Canon* does not tell the story of his life. It was written so his followers would remember forever what they regarded as most important — Buddha's ideas and teachings. Even so, you can find out about him from other kinds of written evidence. Before you begin your work, however, you need to think about the following problem.

Sometimes, people who write about a great person try to show just how important this person will be for the world. To do this they may use events or words in a way that will show just how special that person is or was. For example, there might have been an unusual light in the sky at the time of a great person's birth. The writer describes this but goes on to suggest that perhaps it was a sign or a symbol of the person's appearance as being as bright as the sun. The writer is trying to give us a feeling of that person's warmth and strength which he or she feels ordinary words cannot explain. So writers may use not only facts but also symbols in giving their opinion and interpretations. Sometimes it is a little difficult to work out which is which.

Now think about the following questions. Do not be afraid to guess. You will not find all the answers in what you have just read.

What difficulties might we have in trying to understand stories about real people who lived long ago?

What difficulties might we have in trying to understand stories written about real people who lived long ago, written by people who also lived long ago?

Think spot

The life history that we are going to use was probably the first and most important one to have been written about the Buddha. It was written in the first century CE by an Indian poet called Ashvaghosha. He called it the *Acts of the Buddha*.

The information for his history probably came from other stories that had been passed down of what Buddha had said and done. As you read it, remember what has been said already about trying to understand stories about people like the Buddha. You will also need to think carefully about the kind of world the poet lived in, and how he would try to describe events for people who lived in his time.

Ashvaghosha begins his life story of the Buddha by describing the Buddha's father and mother:

> There once lived a king of the Shakyas whose name was Shuddhodana. He was pure in conduct and beloved of the Shakyas like the autumn moon. He had a wife splendid, beautiful and true and she was called the Great Maya.

The poet tells of the love these two have for each other and how Maya realises one day that she is pregnant. Unlike many pregnant women, Maya does not suffer from tiredness. Ashvaghosha says:

> She set her heart on going to Lumbini, a small wood, with trees of every kind.... She asked the King to go with her, and so they left the city and went to that glorious place.
>
> When the Queen noticed that the time of her delivery was approaching, she went to a couch overspread with an awning, thousands of waiting women looking on with joy in their hearts. The lucky stars of the constellation Pushya shone brightly when a son was born to the Queen for the good of the world.

Ashvaghosha then goes on to describe the birth of the child:

> He came out of his mother's side, without causing her pain or injury.... He did not enter the world in the usual way, and he appeared like someone descended from the sky.... When born, he was so lustrous and true that it appeared as if the young sun had come down to earth. And yet when people gazed at his dazzling brilliance he held their eyes like the moon. His limbs shone with the brightness of gold, and lit up all the space around.

According to Ashvaghosha the child took seven long steps and told those present that he had been born for the good of all that lived. An old man was there who could foresee the future and he began to cry. Ashvaghosha explains that the man was not crying for the child but for himself. He could foretell that the child would give up everything but that he would find the way to stop the process of being reborn. In this he would put an end to personal suffering. The man cried because he knew that he would not live to see it happen.

Ashvaghosha now returns to the Queen and her son:

Queen Maya could not bear the joy which she felt at the sight of her son's majesty.... So she went to heaven, to dwell there. Her sister, his aunt, then brought up the prince as if he were her own son.

His childhood passed without serious illness.... In a few days he acquired the knowledge required by a prince. Normally this takes years to learn.

The boy's name was Siddhartha Gautama. His father, the King, was worried by the old man's prediction that his son would give up everything, including his kingdom. So he made sure that Siddhartha led a very private life inside his palace. Then his father decided that one way to keep Siddhartha occupied was to marry him off to a beautiful young princess!

His father selected for him...a maiden, Yashodara by name...outstanding for her beauty, modesty, and good breeding.... And the prince, wondrous in his flashing beauty, took his delight with the bride chosen for him by his father...in the course of time Yashodara bore a son, who was named Rahula.

Copy the table below. Under each of the headings write the information or ideas that you think best fit those headings.
One possible fact and one possible symbol have already been written in as examples. But you must decide what the symbol means.

Think spot

Possible facts of Gautama's life	Symbols or signs used by the poet	Meanings
His mother, Queen Maya, went to the Lumbini gardens.	The young sun	....

The poet wrote his life history long after Siddhartha had died. He knew, therefore, what had happened to him and how his life had influenced many people.

Is there anything that you have read so far which shows how the beginning of a story could be influenced by knowing how it ends?

Think spot

Think spot

Look at the two pictures showing part of a story about Siddhartha's early life.

How do you know who Siddhartha is in each of the pictures?

In the first picture the child Siddhartha's footsteps become lotus flowers. Can you guess what the lotus flowers might mean?

What event do you think is taking place in the second picture?

3

The prince's world

We have learned something of Siddhartha's birth from the poet Ashvaghosha. Now we will try to give you some information about the kind of kingdom Siddhartha's father ruled, what the people were like and what they believed.

The kingdom

You will need to remember that Siddhartha lived long ago, perhaps over 2500 years ago. At that time, people in Northern India lived mainly in small groups, clans or tribes. Siddhartha's father ruled a tribe called the Shakyas. They lived in the hills that lead up to the Himalayan mountains in Northern India. This part of India is called Nepal. You can see it on the map. Siddhartha's family name was Gautama just as your family's name might be Jones or Smith. The people probably farmed and lived in small villages. Siddhartha's family seemed to have lived in a town.

The people's beliefs

Everyone in the community belonged to a group, or *caste*. Each caste had its own rules and way of life. Some castes were thought to be more important than others, and a person from one caste was not allowed to marry someone from a different caste, except for very special reasons. The most important caste was the *Brahmin*. Brahmins were called the 'gods on earth'. They were the only ones who could carry out religious ceremonies.

   Most of the people believed in many different gods, but there were some who also thought that one god was responsible for all creation. One important belief was that whatever you did had its consequences. If you did good it would bring good results in the future and so on. These good or bad results were called *Karma*. Many people also believed that you could be reborn as another person or living thing and that what you became would depend on how good or bad a life you had led before. Being reborn in this way was called *Samsara*. People did not think that you had to go on being reborn forever. They hoped that they would eventually be able to live such a good life that they would stop being reborn and so all their suffering would be ended.

Difficult times

When Siddhartha was born, India was going through a time of great change. New kingdoms were ruled over by kings who had conquered the smaller kingdoms and made them part of larger ones. People were fearful for the future. They did not know what might happen to them or their families. New rulers meant new laws and customs. Many people began to question the meaning of their own lives and life in general. After all, it is sometimes difficult to feel that there is any point in living when your life is filled with violence and disease. They wanted to know *why* it was that troubles and suffering could happen to people who had done no wrong. Some were so unhappy with what was happening to them that they felt that their beliefs and religious customs could not help them any more.

Of course there were people who tried to answer these very difficult questions. Some said you could overcome your problems if you gave up all that others called the pleasures of life. In this way you would be able to control the body and mind. All difficulties could then be ignored or put on one side. Others argued that as life was so short you should live it to the full and not think about the consequences. Many people felt, however, that they needed more than these two ways could offer.

It was into this uncertain world that Siddhartha Gautama was born and in which he was expected to rule as a king when his father died.

This has been a lot of information to take in at one go. Read it through again, and then try to use what you have remembered to do the next task *without* going back to the information.

Think spot

Here are some sentences. Decide whether they are accurate or not. If you think that they are not accurate, write down what you think is the right information.
1   During Siddhartha's time people believed in only one god.
2   Everyone believed that death was not the end.
3   Karma means being reborn.
4   Samsara means doing good and evil things.
5   The reason why people felt unhappy was because their sacrifices could only be made by the Brahmins.
6   No one had any suggestions as to how people might deal with violence and suffering in their lives.

Now compare your sentences with a friend. If you find that you have different answers, try to find out the reasons for your differences.

Then check all your findings against the information given earlier.

As a prince, Siddhartha would have led an easy life. Shuddhodana, however, is said to have made extra special arrangements to prevent his son from seeing what the world outside his palace was like. The poet says that the king:

> arranged for him (Siddhartha) *to live in the upper storeys of the palace. Thus he passed his time in the upper parts of the palace, which was as brilliantly white as rain clouds in autumn and which looked like a great house of the gods slipped to earth. It contained rooms suited to each season, and the melodious music of female attendants could be heard in them. . . . And it did not occur to him to come down from the palace to the ground, just as people who in reward for their goodness live in a palace in heaven and are happy to remain there, and have no desire to come down to earth.*

A little later in the life history we learn that the king is determined that his son should know nothing about old age, poverty, disease or death.

Imagine that you have a friend who has been protected in this way. How would you explain fully and truthfully the meaning of these pictures that he has found in a magazine?

Think spot

List the questions that you think your friend would ask. Write out your explanations or talk about them with a partner. How do you think your friend would feel when he hears what you have to say about each of the pictures?

Of course you can always keep a person away from the outside world but it is difficult to stop people from talking about it. According to the poet the ladies of the palace talked about some beautiful trees and places that they knew of outside the palace and the city. Siddhartha said that he too wanted to visit them. His father gave in but not before he had given orders for all the sick, poor, old and dying to be removed from the road that Siddhartha would take. Unfortunately, in spite of all his care, an old man appeared on the road. Just like anyone seeing something new and strange, Siddhartha asked for an explanation and his charioteer tried to give him one:

The prince's charioteer explained the meaning of old age and he was shocked.... 'So that is how old age destroys the memory, beauty and strength of every one. And yet no one seems to worry about it. This being so turn round the horses, and travel quickly to our palace. How can I delight to walk about in parks when my heart is full of the fear of ageing?'

It was not long before Siddhartha decided to leave the palace again. This time in spite of all the care that had been taken, a sick person crossed his path. This is how the poet described Siddhartha's reaction:

When this fact (sickness) was explained to him he was dismayed, and trembled like the reflection of the moon on rippling water. Again he was shocked to find that the diseases of others did not seem to disturb people or prevent them from enjoying themselves. He returned home.

Even so, the young prince found that he still wished to leave the palace. Once more he saw something that he had never seen before. It was a body being taken for burning. This was the first time that he had seen a dead person and now he was to learn that death came to every person. So the charioteer

again explained the meaning of the sight to the prince. Courageous though he was, the king's son was suddenly filled with dismay. He called out, 'This is the end which has been fixed for all and yet the world forgets its fears and takes no notice. Turn back the chariot! This is no time or place for pleasure outings.'

From that moment on the young prince could find no happiness in his palace. He decided to leave the palace once more. This time he watched the people at work and was shocked at what he saw. He could see their suffering and the suffering of the animals that they used. He could not understand why other people did not seem to be as sad as he was at the way in which others had to suffer. Siddhartha had many questions that he wanted to ask. Why did people

11

have to live, suffer and die? What was the meaning of it all? How could he begin to find the answers to such questions? The poet tells us that it was now that a wandering holy man met Siddhartha. He told Siddhartha that he too had wondered about the meaning of life. In fact he had now given up his home and lived on the charity of others so that he could pass all his time in trying to find the answers which would free him from the world forever.

Siddhartha, however, was rich. He had a loving family, one day he would be a king — what was *he* to do? He knew as soon as he had heard the old man's story.

Think spot What do you think Siddhartha decided that he should do? Put your ideas down on a piece of paper.

The poet tells us:

He made plans to leave his palace for the homeless life. And soon after returning to his palace he decided to escape during the night. He woke Chandaka the groom and ordered him quickly to bring the horse Kanthaka. 'For I want to depart from here today, and win the deathless state.'

In this picture you can see Siddhartha leaving home. How can you tell that people do not want him to go?

In this picture you can see what Siddhartha did next. Here is what the poet says is Siddhartha's own explanation.

Not long after, although I was young I cut off my hair and beard, put on the yellow robes against the wishes of my weeping parents and I went from home to homelessness.

There could be no doubt that Siddhartha was serious. Hair that was long and cared for and a good beard were signs of a rich person. It was clear what Siddhartha meant when he cut them off. The yellow robes were the kind of robes that were put on the bodies of the dead. Siddhartha was making the point that he was now dead to his family and one of the poor. He was about to begin a journey in which he would try to find the meaning of his existence. The difficulty was to know how to begin the journey. This was not to be a journey that would take him across the world, although he knew that he had to leave his home. No, this was to be a journey into the mysteries of his own mind!

Think spot

With a friend, try to think of all the arguments that Siddhartha's father and mother might have used to try to stop him leaving. Then work out how Siddhartha might have tried to reply to them.

Do you think that Siddhartha would have had the same feelings if he had been a poor person?

Do you think that Siddhartha would have had the same feelings if his father had not tried to keep him away from the world?

Don't forget to give reasons for all your answers and don't be afraid to guess.

Before we go any further perhaps we should just think about the life history itself. It was written a long time after the death of Siddhartha.

You have already thought about what that might mean for people reading it now. People will have different ideas about how the description of what happened when he left the palace should be interpreted.

Here are four possible ideas.

1   Some will think that each part of the story happened just as the poet has written it down.
2   Others will think that Siddhartha met many people who were sick, poor and dying. They will feel that the poet has chosen to use examples of such people.
3   There will be those who think that the poet is using the four people as *symbols* of those things that are part of every human being's life history.
4   Some people will think that parts of 1, 2 and 3 are possible. So they will feel that the events described did happen but that the poet has picked them out to act as symbols as well.

Think spot

Do you have any other ideas?

Of the ways mentioned above, is there one that you prefer? If so, why?

14

4

Finding the way

The statue shown in this picture tells us a little of what happened at the beginning of Siddhartha's journey. He wanted to find the answer to one big question in particular:

how could a man escape the weariness of existence and suffering?

In order to find the answer, he joined up with two men called Alara Kalama and Udda-ka Ramaputta. He thought that they would be able to teach him the kinds of things he could do that would help him to think deeply about the problem. With five other men he learned how to concentrate deeply. Nowadays we call it *meditation*. He also fasted, taking in just enough food to keep him alive. At last he reached the state shown in the picture.

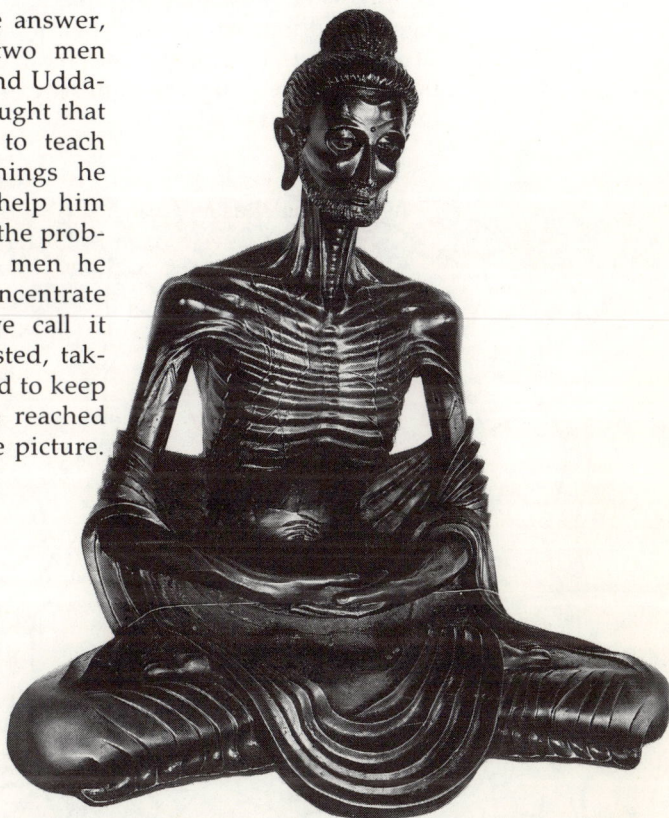

Study the picture. Write down as clear and accurate a description as you can. Then go on to say how you feel about the picture. You may find it useful to imagine that you are trying to describe it to a person who cannot see it.

Think spot

This way of life, which involves doing without food and any form of pleasure, is called *asceticism* and Siddhartha lived in this way for six years. It became clear to him, however, that he would never be able to find the answer to his questions if he went on fasting. He was becoming nothing more than skin and bones and it was obvious that:

this kind of self torture merely wore out his body without any useful result. He said, 'I must take steps to increase the strength of this body. When that is worn down and exhausted by hunger and thirst, the mind in its turn must feel the strain. . . . Only when the body is reasonably fed can undue strain on the mind be avoided.'

The life history explains that he decided to bathe in the river before he took his first proper meal. He was so weak that he found it difficult to climb back up the river's bank. As he rested a young girl passed by. She stopped and begged Siddhartha to take her milk rice and from it he gained the strength to go on. His five friends, however, felt that he had given up the right way to find the answer to his questions and they left him.

Siddhartha made his way to a holy fig tree. He then sat cross-legged, which is the best position of all because it prevents movement. And he said to himself, 'I shall not change this my position so long as I have not done what I have set out to do.'

5

The road to enlightenment

If and when Siddhartha found what he was looking for he would have *Bodhi*, or perfect knowledge. In other words he would have answers to all his questions. Clearly it would not be easy to find, and Siddhartha would need to concentrate very hard in order to reach the right state of meditation.

Think spot

Think about when and where you find it best to concentrate very hard on what you are doing. Now think about all the things that prevent you from concentrating.

List all the things that you think might have prevented Siddhartha from meditating.

We are told in the story of Siddhartha that a truly evil being called Mara tried to disturb him. People called Mara the god of love but they were very afraid of what he did to them. Ashvaghosha tells us what happens next:

People dread Mara as one who hates the very thought of freedom. He had with him three sons, Flurry, Gaiety and Sullen Pride, and his three daughters, Discontent, Delight and Thirst. They asked Mara why he was so upset, and he replied, 'Look over there at that wise man...he has sat down with a first intention of conquering my kingdom. No wonder that I am so unhappy. If he should succeed in overcoming me my kingdom will be empty. But so far he has not yet found Bodhi. He is still under my influence. While in due time I will try to break his solemn purpose, and throw myself against him like a rush of a river in flood breaking against its bank.'

This picture shows Mara's attempt to distract Siddhartha.

Think spot

With a partner, list all the ways with which Mara might try to disturb Siddhartha's meditation. Remember Mara's children, as their names may give you some clues as to what he might try. It's also useful to think about what Mara says. It may give a clue as to what kind of god he might be when forced to do something about an enemy.

Whatever happened to Siddhartha it could not stop him from going into a deep trance. Then we are told something began to happen.

The first watch

In the first watch of the night (from 6 o'clock to 10) Siddhartha found that he knew about his previous lives. He said, 'There I was so and so; that was my name; dead there, I came here'. In this way he remembered the thousands of births as though he were living them over again. When he had seen all his own births and deaths he thought of other living beings and thought to himself, 'Again and again they must leave people they think of as their own, and must go on elsewhere, and that without ever stopping. Surely this world is unprotected and helpless, and like a wheel it goes round and round.'

Think for a moment about what you have just read. Now try to answer the following question:

Do you think that Siddhartha was made happy or unhappy by what he saw in his mind?

Siddhartha uses a wheel as a symbol for the idea that people are born, die and are reborn. Imagine that you have been asked to show this idea in a picture or a design. How would you do it? You may either draw the picture or design yourself or tell someone else your ideas so that he or she can do it for you.

Now read what happened next.

The second watch

During the second watch (from 10 o'clock to 2 in the morning) he saw that the death and rebirth of all living things depended on whether they had done good or bad things during their lifetimes. He saw that the threat of death is always present and that creatures could never find a resting place.

You sometimes hear people say that the 'only certain thing in life is that everyone has to die'. During Roman times when a great general entered Rome as a hero, a man was paid to stand with him in the chariot. The man's job was to whisper in the hero's ear, 'Remember, thou art mortal.' In other words, you might feel like a god but you too have to die like everyone else. If you look at some of the tombs in churches in this country you can sometimes find a skull or a skeleton carved out. These are called *memento mori*. They are just another way of reminding everyone that death is always present.

Do you think that the idea of death always being part of life:
(a) helps people to act in ways that are good rather than bad;
(b) makes people cram as many experiences into their lives as they can because life is short;
(c) tends to make people very selfish, wanting only to get the best of things for themselves;
(d) means that no matter where they go or what they do people cannot avoid the process of dying, or
(e) makes people do many different things that will prevent them from thinking about it?

You may decide that more than one of the ideas are important for you. Make a list of them and any others that you might think of. Then compare your list with a friend.

Which, if any, of these ideas do you think Siddhartha would have found to be good descriptions of what he was learning in the second watch?

Even after the second watch, Siddhartha had not seen all that he needed to if he were to have perfect knowledge.

The third watch

Then as the third watch drew on (from 2 o'clock to 6 in the morning) he thought, 'Alas, all living things wear themselves out. Over and over again they are born, they age and die, pass on to a new life, and are reborn. What is more, greed and false hopes blind them and they are blind from birth. Frightened, they do not yet know how to get out of this great ill!' Siddhartha found that lack of self knowledge was the key. Once you understood what caused all the problems that happened to living creatures, including yourself, and through that knew how to live your life, then birth, death and illness all would cease.

Then Siddhartha had achieved a correct knowledge of all there is to be known, and he stood out in the world as a Buddha.

Think spot

In the picture below Stephen, aged 11, has tried to show what the Buddha had discovered. What symbols has he used? Discuss with a friend how well you think Stephen has brought out the meaning.

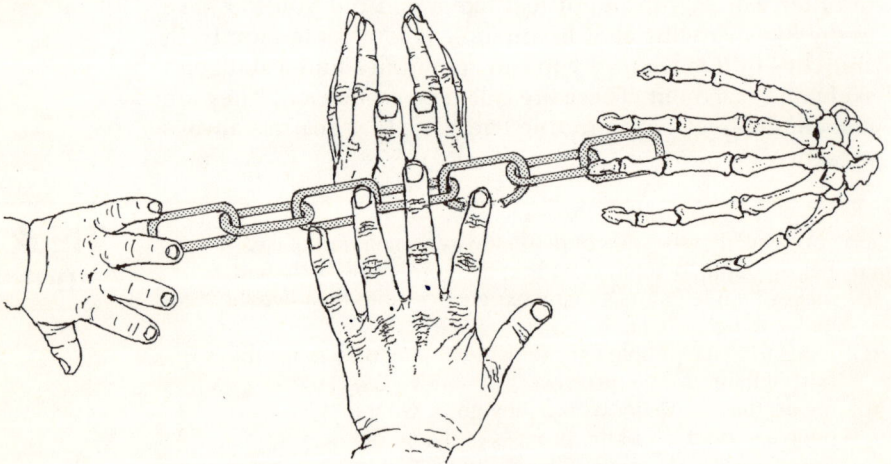

The fourth watch

All living things rejoiced and sensed that all went well. Mara alone felt deep displeasure. For seven days Siddhartha, the Buddha, stayed. His body gave him no trouble, his eyes never closed and he looked into his own mind. He thought, 'Here I have found freedom.'

6

The Buddha

From now on we shall call Siddhartha Gautama only by his
new title, the Buddha. The word means the 'enlightened
one', or the one who has perfect knowledge. Can you
remember the other word from which this one might come?

If you are enlightened it means that you know all that you
need to know about something. You are no longer ignorant.
It's like having part of your mind light up so that what was
not clear to you is now absolutely clear. The Buddha's mind

was no longer 'in the dark'. Everything was clear. He knew not only *how* things happened but *why* they happened.

Enlightenment, then, is seeing things as they really are without other things getting in the way or making them seem different from what they are. The truth of anything is like the sun or the moon; it is always there, even though on occasions it cannot be seen for clouds.

The truth, or perfect knowledge, is called *Dharma*. It is always there, has always been there and always will be there to be uncovered. Buddha had discovered it for himself, as others had done in the past and as others will do in the future.

Think spot

Now the Buddha was fully awakened to how things really are, his next decision was about what to do with this knowledge. Should he:

(a) continue to meditate;
(b) decide not to teach other people about what he had found out because it would be too difficult for them to understand;
(c) go back to his palace and family and work hard to improve the lives of his people;
(d) teach other people about all the ideas he had discovered; or
(e) teach other people so that they could spread the ideas for him?

Put these five suggestions in the order that you think shows what the Buddha ought to have done. For example, you might think that (c) is the most important thing, followed by (a). So your list would begin: (c), (a). . .

When you have completed your list, ask two friends to show you their lists. Explain to them why you have made your particular choices. Then ask them to tell you why they have made their choices. Even if you have made the same choices you may find that your reasons are different.

After your discussion, choose from your own list the thing that you think the Buddha actually did.

Perhaps you can work out what the Buddha decided to do from the following:

Having myself crossed the ocean of suffering I must help others to cross it. Freed myself, I must set others free. This is the promise which I have made in the past when I saw all that lives in distress.

The Buddha believed that all he had discovered during his meditation should be passed on to other people. He saw, however, that they would find it hard to understand the things that he had found out. This meant that he would have to spend the rest of his life teaching. It also meant that he would have to find ways of teaching that would make

his ideas so clear that anyone who wanted to could understand and follow them.

After his Enlightenment the Buddha decided to go to
Benares. There, in the Deer Park, he met the five men who
had been with him when he had been an ascetic (see p.15).
They were still shocked to find that he no longer starved
himself, but they could see that there was something different about him. He was confident and they were prepared
to listen to him.

How do you think he answered their criticism that he no longer
acted like a proper holy man should?
Look back at p.16 to help you find the answer.

**Think
spot**

After the Buddha had explained to the five men how he
had been able to discover perfect knowledge, he then went
on to tell them what it was he had uncovered. This is called
the *Four Noble Truths*. We shall explore what these truths
mean in the next chapter.

7
Showing the way

There are many ideas about what the Buddha actually taught, and different countries and peoples have various ways of explaining and remembering them. Even so, all those who follow the Buddha do agree on certain basic teachings. These are known as the *Four Noble Truths*. It was the Four Noble Truths that Buddha is believed to have taught in the Deer Park near Benares.

The Buddha's way of looking at the world was like that of a doctor. First of all he observed what was happening to all living things. He found that suffering was part of everyone's life. Then he diagnosed what were the causes of suffering. Lastly he prescribed the way in which people could bring the causes of suffering to an end for themselves.

The First Noble Truth: Dukkha

The Buddha called the First Noble Truth, *Dukkha*. This word is difficult to translate into English. One way of putting it would be that life is generally unsatisfactory. He thought that there were three ways in which this could be seen.

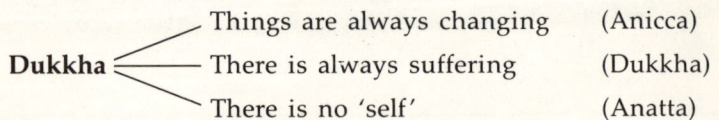

Dukkha — Things are always changing (Anicca)
— There is always suffering (Dukkha)
— There is no 'self' (Anatta)

Things are always changing

Think spot

Imagine that you are observing the world in a similar way to the Buddha. Here are some pictures of the kind of things you might see.

1 Explain to a partner what is being shown by each pair of pictures.
2 Write a caption or title for each pair.

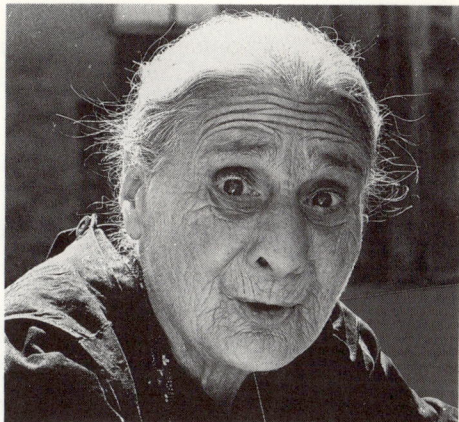

Each pair of pictures has to do with pain or suffering, the kind of pain or suffering that happens in every person's life.

The Buddha said that some kinds of suffering happen because everything must change. The young grow old, famines can follow good harvests and healthy cells in the body can change and cause a deadly growth. There is, however, another kind of suffering that the Buddha described. The next Think Spot will help you to discover what it is.

There is always suffering

1 With a partner, discuss the thoughts and feelings of the people in these pictures.
2 Describe how those people might feel later on when looking at the pictures.

Like the Buddha, you will probably have realised that even times of great happiness must give way to feelings of being less happy. Perhaps you have had a moment when you felt really happy. What happened when the moment was over? Did you feel let down for no reason at all? Perhaps people said that you had been overexcited, overtired, difficult to please, or that you were just being silly. The Buddha understood this feeling of being let down. He saw that you could not go on living the same moment. It's rather like being a mountaineer. It's marvellous reaching the top of the mountain but you cannot stay there forever. Unfortunately coming down is not quite the same thing.

There is no 'self'

We have found out something about two of the things that bring about Dukkha. Now we are going to look at a third. Buddha called it *Anatta* which means without self, or *No-I*.

This is the part of the Buddha's teaching that was, and is, the most different from many other religions. Buddha knew this and wondered if he could teach it to other people. In the end, he said the world is like a lotus pond. In the lotus pond some of the lotus plants are under the water, some have just risen to the top and others stand above the water. The world is like the pond and the people in it are all at different stages. Some would be ready to understand the Truth that he was about to tell them. So the Buddha decided to teach about the third cause of suffering.

Buddha's teaching was that we are all what we think, see, feel, touch, and smell. All these things added together make us. Once these stop happening so do we. There is nothing left. When we die, our bodies disintegrate and there is nothing left that can be described as being *us* left over.

To illustrate this idea, look at something like a bike. It can be broken down into its basic parts, axle, wheels, tyres, rims, chain, cogs and so on. Once you have taken a bike apart it does not exist any more. All that remains is a pile of parts. Even so, these parts can be used to make new bikes or other machines so, although the original bike has gone, its elements can be used to make new and different things.

Buddha knew that this idea would frighten people if they could not be taught to understand it. The question is why should they feel this way. Here are some suggestions:

The idea of Anatta is not easy for people to understand. Many people believe in a god or in gods. In many religions this belief means that the people feel special. They hope that they will be rewarded for their belief and the good things that they do as a result of those beliefs with some kind of life after death. In other words, although they might not be the same as they are now, the thing that makes them the person they are will go on. In some religions this 'something' is called the soul, in others it may be called the spirit. So it is not too hard to see why such people would find the Buddha's teaching rather difficult to accept.

There are other people, however, who do not believe in any kinds of gods or god. They do not believe that there is some kind of heaven or hell, life after death, soul or spirit. Yet they say there is still something that makes each person what they are. No matter what happens to you, there is something within you that is never changed. If you like, it is the **you** of you. It was there at your birth and remains throughout your life.

The Buddha believed that all the time people thought that they were permanent in some way or other they would suffer. If they could give up that way of looking at things then they would know peace and happiness.

Think spot

Two people who have only just started to find out about the teachings of Buddha have ended up with two different ideas about what might happen if people believed in Anatta.
1 People who believe in Anatta might become more selfish about getting things like money, cars, expensive house, clothes and holidays, and so on. It would encourage them to think only about making the best of a short life. There would be no point in doing good deeds because there would not be any reward in the future.

2 People who believe in Anatta might learn to become less greedy and selfish. They might think that they should try to make the world a better and more caring place to live in for everyone. It would not be a comfortable place just for the few. People would learn to do good deeds and to behave properly without thinking that there is something in it for them.

With a partner discuss the two conclusions above.
Do you:
(a) agree with either of the conclusions;
(b) disagree with either of the conclusions;
(c) agree with parts of both of them;
(d) disagree with parts of both of them; or
(e) want to wait until you have found out a bit more about Buddha's teaching?

Think spot

Since the word Dukkha has more than one meaning, when talking about Buddhism should you:
(a) use the word Dukkha;
(b) use an English translation, e.g. suffering; or
(c) use a whole sentence to explain each time?

Give reasons for your answer.

The Second Noble Truth: the cause of suffering

If you decided not to make a decision until you had found out more about the Buddha's teaching then you have probably acted wisely!

On p.24 we said that the Buddha was a like a good doctor. He had found that suffering exists for everyone and his next task was to find what caused it. He believed that you could not help people until you knew the causes of their

29

difficulties. Buddha had seen the outward signs of what was wrong. This he called *impermanence*, which is another way of saying that everything changes. But what lay behind the idea of impermanence that caused suffering?

The Buddha said that the First Noble Truth is that the suffering and pain that comes because everything has to change is caused by one thing. He saw that people were always wanting pleasure and happiness. They can never get enough, however, and so they go on wanting more. Buddha described it as *Tanha*, which means a kind of thirst or craving. Wanting happiness is rather like being very hot during a heat wave. You keep on drinking iced drinks and for a short while you feel satisfied. Then the effects wear off and you find you want another iced drink. Of course, there are people who encourage you to want many different things, all of which are supposed to make you feel happy. Look at these adverts. No doubt you can think of other ones. Even the countries in which we live teach us to want certain things and encourage us to work for them.

The Buddha said that when you looked closely at what made people want in this way you found three reasons: **greed**, **hatred**, and **not being able to see things as they really are**. Another way of describing that last reason is **lack of knowledge**. This wanting, or thirst, is so strong that it also leads to wanting to be born so that the process can be gone through all over again. It's like a never-ending circle from which there is no escape. This circle is called *Samsara*, or the Cycle of Existence.

Think spot

In this picture you will see how followers of Buddha sometimes show the three reasons for wanting. Which animal is the symbol for which reason? If you were making new symbols for today what would you choose and how would you show them?

The First Noble Truth shows that the causes of suffering are wanting, greed, hatred and not being able to see things as they really are. Buddha described these things as 'fires'. Why do you think he used that particular description?

The Buddha said certain things about Anatta which show that being born again does not mean that a person comes back after death. Look back to p.28 and see if you can work out why. Now try to work out with a friend what you think is meant by being born again when you have to take into account the idea of Anatta.

Look at the adverts again and then go on to answer the questions below.

Think spot

1 Do you think people can be made happy by owning the things shown in the pictures?
   Give reasons for your ideas.

2 What do you think Buddha would say to someone who said that they would be happy to have the things shown in the adverts?

Karma and rebirth

Just what did the Buddha mean when he talked about being born again? In the First Noble Truth we found out that he said that when people died nothing of them was left. When we are alive we are a collection of things and feelings. All of these work together but when we die we fall apart. Each part disintegrates until there is nothing left to show what we were like originally. We said that it's like being a bike. The wheels are taken off, their rims are removed, the spokes and axles are broken down. Each part of the bike is taken away until finally there is nothing to show what the bike was like. Of course, the parts can be used elsewhere but what made the bike that particular bike has gone forever.

The Buddha, therefore, said that there is nothing of the person that is passed on. He taught that it is *Karma* that brings rebirth. Karma is the result of all the thoughts and behaviour of any one person. Good actions and good thoughts will result in good Karma. Bad thoughts and bad actions will bring bad Karma. So it is the *effects* of a person's Karma and not the person or some part of the person, which goes on after the person has died.

How?

Remember that in rebirth nothing is passed on except the effects of the Karma. Imagine a marble being flicked by a finger and thumb. The marble hits another marble and stops. The second marble, however, spins off in the direction that the force of the first marble has sent it. It cannot control itself. So the Buddha says when you die the Karma that you have made through all your actions and thoughts provides the force which gives another living thing the direction for its life. If the Karma is bad then the direction will be bad. If the Karma is good then the direction will be good.

Think spot   Can you think of other ways in which this idea of Karma could be explained to someone else?

Think spot   Think about the following and write down what you think are possible answers.

A little boy is told by his mother to give some of his pocket money to a charity. Is the action of the mother an example of creating good Karma?

When the little boy gives the money to charity, is that an example of creating good Karma?

The Third Noble Truth:
the cause of suffering can be ended

In the Third Noble Truth Buddha showed that the cause of suffering could be brought to an end. People would have to stop thinking and behaving in ways that made them want to cling to life. All the time that they thought that living was precious, Karma would be created. No matter what they did, whether it was good or bad, any desire to go on living would be part of Karma and it was Karma which brought about *Samsara*, or rebirth.

This longing or desire for life is often described as a fire or a flame, which will be blown out when the person has overcome wanting to continue. When a person has managed to do this he has reached the state of *Nirvana*.

Anyone who reaches a state of Nirvana no longer thinks or acts selfishly. They are totally free and at peace with themselves and the world. When they die their Karma ceases to exist. People who are on the way to finding this freedom for themselves will be happy. This is why when Buddhists greet each other they say, 'Sabbe satta sukhita hondu,' which means, 'May all beings be happy.'

The Fourth Noble Truth: the prescription

In the First, Second and Third Noble Truths, Buddha had observed the world's illness and he had *diagnosed* the cause of the illness. Now in the Fourth Noble Truth, he was to give the *prescription*, or the way in which people could cure the illness and achieve Nirvana.

We have found out from the work we have done so far that Buddha taught that:
1 Nothing is fixed or permanent in the world; everything and everybody changes.
2 We are all made up of parts. When these are taken away or broken down, nothing that was us remains. When we die, nothing of ourselves continues. It is only the Karma that we have created that gives direction to other beings' future lives.
3 Suffering is part of all creatures' lives. You may be happy and joyful for a while but it cannot last.
4 There is a way to end suffering.

The prescription that Buddha gave the world is called the *Eightfold Path* by the Buddhists. It shows the way in which people can find and cure the cause of suffering. Then they can put out the fire of wanting and attain Nirvana. Again it is impossible to find an English word which means the same as Nirvana. Buddhists say that Nirvana cannot be talked about, it can only be experienced.

Think spot

With a partner:
(a) make a diagnosis of what you feel is wrong with the world today. For example, you might decide there is too much violence in the world.
(b) prescribe eight ways or ideas that you think would put the world right. For example, your prescription might be to ban all those things that show violence as exciting or pleasurable.

When you have completed your list go to the next chapter and read what the Buddha prescribed.

8

The Eightfold Path

The Buddha had made one very important discovery. He said that the cause of suffering came in the end from peoples' idea that they were special. If you feel different from all other things then you will always be concerned with doing things that give you pleasure. You will also try to avoid anything that will cause you discomfort. Your life will be a search for ease and safety. You will only do what you want to or have things as you want them to be. Of course you are not always successful in getting what you want and so you suffer. Often other people suffer too as a result of your actions. This means that people find it difficult to live not only with other people but also with animals and plants. In other words they affect the environment in which they live.

The energy for all this behaviour comes from the three things mentioned on p.30. These are hatred, greed and lack of knowledge. Somehow each person has to stop thinking and feeling special and to overcome their greed, hatred and lack of knowledge. The Buddha said that this could be done by following the *Eightfold Path*.

In fact, the Eightfold Path is eight ways of behaving. All of them have to be followed because each one depends on the other if the person is to be successful in becoming free from all selfish behaviour and actions.

You can divide the Eightfold Path into three parts.

1 Right seeing and understanding ⎫
2 Right thought   ⎬ Wisdom

3 Right speech   ⎫
4 Right action   ⎬ Morality
5 Right livelihood ⎭

6 Right effort   ⎫
7 Right mindfulness   ⎬ Meditation
8 Right concentration ⎭

On the next page you will find examples of each part of the Path. Before you go on can you work out some examples for yourself?

Can you give examples which will show how some of our actions have a bad effect on animals and the environment?

Think spot

Nirvana

7 Right mindfulness and
8 Right concentration

These two parts of the Path are about meditation. The Buddha had discovered the Four Noble Truths through meditation. He saw it as the way in which others could find out about themselves and the world they lived in. Above all it was the way to Enlightenment and so Nirvana. Any one can begin to meditate. You have to find a comfortable place, sit down, possibly crosslegged and concentrate on your own breathing. If things disturb your peace all that you need to do is to allow them to pass. Gradually you will only be aware of yourself. The more you practise the more you will come to understand the process of meditation.

5 Right livelihood

To follow this part of the path you may not earn a living or do any work which might cause harm or hurt to other beings.

3 Right speech

This requires that you do not say things that you do not mean. You must not tell lies under any circumstances.

1 Right seeing and understanding

This is the most important part of the path. It means that unless you understand or see that the Four Noble Truths are right then you cannot begin to rid yourself of suffering. You have to see the truth that Buddha had discovered. If you accept the Four Noble Truths the rest of the Path can be followed.

6 Right effort

If all the other parts of the Path described so far are followed then people should behave better towards other living things. They should also start to think less about themselves. Even so, they will need to work hard at doing all that is required by the Path. With right effort people can reach the state of Nirvana, although it is a hard and difficult journey.

4 Right action

This means that you must not steal from anyone or anything. You may not cause harm or violence to any living thing, including yourself.

2 Right thought

If you follow Buddha's teaching then you must see things as they really are and not as you would like them to be. For example, if someone does better than you in examinations or a competition you will accept it as a fact. You will not seek ways to explain away your failure or make little of the other person's success.

Start here

What did the Buddha mean by his Eightfold Path? In some ways it is a Path that is easy to understand but, of course, people find it hard to follow.

On the opposite page you will find explanations of each part of the Eightfold Path. Read them carefully. Then look at your own prescriptions for the world's problems. Are any of them like those shown in the Eightfold Path? If they are make a list showing in which part of the Path they belong.

Now think about what you have read and with a friend discuss the following questions. Write down any decisions that you make.
1   Is it possible to follow some of the Eightfold Path without believing in the Four Noble Truths?
2   If you believe in the Buddha's teachings, what jobs might you not be able to do?
3   In what ways might the followers of Buddha's teachings behave towards animals and the environment?
4   What do you think a follower of Buddha would think about war?
5   If your school were to live by the Eightfold Path, in what ways do you think it would be changed?
6   Which do you think is the most important of the Buddha's teachings?
7   Is there any particular teaching that you find interesting? If there is, what is it and why do you find it interesting?
8   If none of the Buddha's teaching interests you can you say why?

Think spot

Now look at the cover of the book. It is a picture of the Buddha and the Dharma.
(a) What do you think the Buddha is holding?
(b) Does it remind you of anything in the life history of the Buddha? If so, what?
(c) What meaning would it have for all the followers of Buddha?
(d) Above the Buddha's head is a lotus flower. This is a symbol for all the Buddha's teaching. There is a monk sitting in the flower. What do you think this is trying to show?

Think spot

37

9

Buddha the teacher

By now you have found out about the most important things that Buddha had to tell other people. But how did he manage to explain such difficult ideas to the many who came to listen to him? Perhaps we should spend a little time trying to answer the question: what makes a good teacher?

On the left-hand side of a piece of paper, list all the words and sentences that you think describe a good teacher. Then ask ten other people whether they agree with any of the words or sentences that you have written down.

Below is part of a list that I have made:

Description	*Number of people who agreed*
1 Is always patient.	****
2 Tells you lots of things.	***
3 Does not bore you.	*****
4 Listens to your ideas.	******

You can see that: 4 out of 10 people agreed with 1;
3 out of 10 people agreed with 2;
5 out of 10 people agreed with 3; and
6 out of 10 people agreed with 4.

It is more than likely that Buddha was a very good teacher, but how can we find out how he taught?

The evidence which shows us what the Buddha taught is to be found in the *Pali Canon*. From these writings, however, we can also find out how he tried to teach other people how to understand his ideas. So when we read the *Pali Canon* we can see that Buddha did the following things:

1 He found out what the people who came to him thought and knew already. Then he would use what they knew to help them to understand new ideas.

2 Buddha explained difficult ideas clearly, in ways that people could follow.

3 He got people to think for themselves and liked them to ask questions.

4 He liked people to test what he said and to learn by doing things and not just listening.

5 Buddha wanted people to meditate as well as to question and argue. In this way they would find the truth within

themselves, as he had done, as well as from others.

The fact that Buddha's ideas continue to be talked about today tells us that the ways he chose to explain them over 2000 years ago must have been successful. You might say that the Buddha was not just a good teacher but a great one!

Think spot

1   Look again at the list of things that the Buddha did when he was teaching. Put them in the order which you think is most important. For example, you might feel that it is more important to do 2 than 3 but that 3 was more important than 4. In the end, therefore, this might be
    2
    3
    4
    1

When you have worked out your own order discuss it with a friend. Remember to give the reasons for your decisions.

2   What do you think the Buddha would have chosen as the most important of the things he did when he taught?

3   Did any of the Buddha's ways of teaching agree with your ideas about what makes a good teacher? If so, which ones?

You have to remember that Buddha's ideas were not only difficult but that they challenged people's ways of thinking about themselves, their lives and their relationship to other living things. The Buddha had no books or pictures to help him put over his ideas. He had to use a method that people were used to and understood. People were used to hearing stories but Buddha's stories were different because they always had a meaning that the listener had to look for. In a way these stories are pictures in words which used events or happenings that people knew about or saw around them. These events and happenings, however, were used by the Buddha as symbols for the new and more difficult ideas that he was trying to teach. We call stories of this kind *parables*.

STORY 1

This story is told by Buddha about a woman who comes to him for advice. The Buddha realises that like many people this woman will only learn through doing something for herself.

The bereaved mother
Once upon a time, said Buddha, there was a poor woman named Gotami. She had a little son who was her pride and joy, but who died when he was four or five years old. She was beside herself

39

with grief, and went from door to door begging her neighbours to tell her of some medicine which would restore her son to life. They only laughed. 'Whoever heard of medicine for the dead?' they asked. Finally she met a wise man who suggested she should go to the Buddha for advice, and this she did, carrying her dead son on her hip. 'You did well,' said the compassionate Buddha, 'to come to me. Go into yonder city and fetch me some grains of mustard seed from a house in which no one has ever died. Then bring them to me and I will see what I can do.'

She went straightaway into the city, still holding her dead son, and called at the first house she came to. 'Yes,' said the kind people who lived there, 'we have plenty of mustard seed. Take what you will.' But when she told them the Buddha had said the seed must come from a house in which no one had ever died, they sighed. They too had lost a little son, about the same age as Gotami's, only a few months before.

Still hopeful, she called at the next house, only to find them mourning the loss of a daughter. In another house people were still grieving over the death of their father, in another their mother; and so it went on. Nowhere in the city was a house to be found which had not suffered the loss of a loved one.

So Gotami took her little son's body to the cremation ground. 'Dear little son,' she said, 'I thought I was alone in my sadness, but now I see that death comes to all men.' So saying, she laid his body on the funeral pyre.

Afterwards she went back to the Buddha. 'Have you brought me the mustard seed?' he asked.

Think spot

How do you think Gotami answered the Buddha? The answer should include what she had learned as a result of looking for the mustard seed.

Here is what happened in the Buddha's version of the story.

'No', she replied. 'I could have brought handfuls of mustard seed, but none of the kind you mentioned. This I have learned from you, Exalted One. Now, I beg you, receive me as one of your disciples so that I may practise meditation with you and learn the truth.'

The Buddha said, 'Blessed are you, my daughter, for you have learned that nothing in this world lasts for ever. Enter my band of holy women and with them follow the Noble Eightfold Path which leads to life.'

So Gotami became a nun and after her death was honoured as a saint.

STORY 2

One day, when the sun was high in the sky and not a breath of wind stirred the dust of the road or the branches of the trees, some followers of Buddha walked out into the countryside. The land shimmered in the heat but the followers did not notice for they were too busy thinking and talking about what the Buddha had taught that morning. As they paused by the side of the road they saw a man coming towards them. It was so hot and bright that at first he appeared to be a long, thin stick. Then as he came into view they could see that he was a workman who made his living from working in the fields. He had already been at work for many hours and would expect to work many more before the day was ended. Hunger and thirst were his constant companions and his eyes were those of a man who earned little and had many mouths to feed. His misery was so obvious to the followers that they set about persuading him to go to Buddha from whom he would hear the Dharma. After that they were sure that he would be a changed man, learning to be at peace with the world and himself.

When they brought the man to the Buddha they pleaded with him to teach the man the Dharma so that he too would be able to free himself from the cycle of rebirth. Buddha, however, listened to the man's silence, greeted him kindly and said to his followers, 'Go now and give our new friend food to eat and water to drink.'

If Dharma is the most important thing in a man's life, why did Buddha decide to feed the man first? You may find the answer in what happened on page 16.

Think spot

There are many people who think that religions should try to answer certain big questions, such as 'How did the world begin? Is there life after death?' and so on.

Here is a story about how the Buddha answered someone who would not become a follower without having an answer to the question, 'Will the world continue forever?'

STORY 3

Suppose a man were pierced with an arrow well steeped in poison, and his close friends and relatives were to summon a doctor or a surgeon. Then suppose the man says, 'I will not have this arrow pulled out until I know of the man by whom I was pierced, both his name and his clan, and whether he be tall or short or of middle stature: till I know whether he be a black man or dark or sallow-skinned: whether he be of such and such a village or suburb or town. I will not have the arrow pulled out until I know of the bow, by which I was pierced, whether it was a long-bow or a cross-bow.

I will not have the arrow pulled out until I know of the bowstring by means of which I was pierced, whether it was made of creeper, or of reed, or of tendon, or of hemp, or of sap-tree.

... Till I know of the arrow by which I have been pierced, whether it be a reed-shaft, or of a sapling.

... Till I know of the feathers of it, whether they be feathers of a vulture or a heron, or of a kite or peacock, or of a hook-bill.

... Till I know of the arrow that has pierced me, whether it is bound with the tendon of an ox or of a buffalo or a deer or a monkey.

... Till I know whether the arrow which has pierced me be just an arrow, or a razor-edge, or a splinter, or a calf-tooth, or a javelin-head, or a barb-headed arrow.'

Think spot
Can you work out what the ending of this story will be?

Now can you work out how this story might answer the question of why Buddha did not spend time on problems like 'How did the world begin?' and so on. Has the story answered the person's question? Give reasons for your answer. When you have written down some of your ideas read on.

The story finishes with the line:

'That man would die without knowing any of these things.'

In the same way anyone who will not follow the Buddha unless he knows the answer to the big questions like 'How did the world begin?' would have to live and die unable to follow the Buddha's way. The Buddha had shown how people might break free from suffering and reach Nirvana. There is no point in finding out about these other things. The man with the arrow would have been saved if he had done the useful thing and pulled it out. The followers of Buddha find freedom if they do the useful thing and follow the Eightfold Path. All the time they ask questions, which will not help to cure the cause of their suffering, they will continue to live unsatisfactory lives (Samsara).

Here is another story. This time the Buddha was trying to explain something about his teachings. Remember each thing in the story is a symbol for something else.

STORY 4

The Buddha said: Just as a man, brethren, who has started on a long journey sees before him a great stretch of water, on this side full of doubts and fears, on the further side safe and free from fears: but there is no boat to cross in, no causeway for passing over from this side to the other side. Then he thinks thus: 'Here is a great stretch of water...but there is no boat. ... How now if I were to gather together grass, sticks, branches and leaves, bind them into a raft, and resting on that raft paddle with hands and feet and so come safe to the further shore?'

Then, brethren, that man gathers together sticks...and comes to the further shore. When he has crossed over and come to the other side he thinks thus: 'This raft has been of great use to me. Resting on this raft and paddling with hand and foot I have come to the further shore. Suppose now I were to set this raft on my head or lift it on to my shoulders and go my ways?'

Now what think ye, brethren? Would that man in so doing have finished with that raft?

First of all write down each of the symbols. By each symbol list what you think it stands for. Your first item might be . . .

Think spot

Symbol	Stands for
Sticks/grass	thoughts, ideas

When you have worked out what each of the symbols might mean can you answer the question of whether the man should leave the raft or take it with him? You will have to think about what the raft stands for in order to answer the question.

This is the way in which Stephen, 12, saw the story's hidden meaning:

The river is the problem.

The sticks are ideas.

The raft is all the ideas becoming a belief.

If he takes the raft with him he will cause another problem.

If he leaves the raft he can always build another one out of more sticks when he reaches another river.

Taking the raft on his shoulder after it has done its duty is a waste of time.

Many small ideas or beliefs mount up into one big one.

To solve his problems he no longer has to use the beliefs but has faith in himself.

With his faith he can conquer most of the problems he now faces on his journey.

Stephen is really thinking out loud. Do you think he is on the right lines? Does it seem to be the same as your way of looking at the story?

Think spot

In fact Stephen seems to be close to what the story means. The river is probably a symbol for life itself. The raft is the Buddha's teaching. The man is the follower of Buddha. In his journey through the problems of life the man has used the Buddha's teaching. Once he has overcome the problems of life, however, and has found peace, Nirvana, he has no further need of the teachings and, like the raft, he can leave them behind.

Perhaps you would like to write a story that has a hidden meaning. This is a story written by Debbie and Robert (aged 12).

Midas was a very rich man. He lived in India in the finest of houses. Some people said he had everything but he knew there was something he did not have. Happiness! One night Midas had a very strange dream.

There were two men walking along a road. They came to a huge pile of gold in the road and the men could not get over it, under it or round it. One of the men started to collect the gold and to put it in a sack. The other stepped off the road and followed a track that led him to the gates of paradise.

When Midas woke up there were tears in his eyes but he did not know why.

Think spot

Can you work out how the story ends and what its meaning might be?
Now try to write one of your own.

10

Journey's end

The Buddha's teachings were for everyone. His father became one of his first followers, and other kings and queens, the rich and the poor all came to listen and to begin the journey along the Eightfold Path. No one was too great or small for the Buddha to approach. He even went onto a battlefield to prevent two warring tribes from killing each other over a question of water rights. At another time he persuaded a king not to conquer another kingdom. No wonder, therefore, that he taught kings about their responsibilities to their subjects and the people their responsibilities to all living things. He tried to show everyone that greed, hatred, intolerance and prejudice had to be overcome if true happiness was to be achieved.

There seems to have been only one person who hated the Buddha. This was a cousin. It is said that the cousin tried to kill Buddha because he was so jealous of the Buddha's success and popularity. The Buddha managed to deal with the attempts on his life and lived to a ripe old age. Apart from this the Buddha seems to have been loved and respected by all.

As time went on, some men and women gave up all thoughts of marriage and family life, joined the Buddha and became his disciples. These were monks and nuns. The monks lived in small groups called the *Sangha*, or community. Like the Buddha they wore saffron coloured robes, lived on the food other people gave them, meditated and learned and taught about the Four Noble Truths and the Eightfold Path.

After 45 years of teaching the Dharma the Buddha knew that his teachings would continue to be taught in the future. The Buddha's followers, however, were not so sure of themselves. They became very worried when, at the age of 80, he fell ill. When he recovered, the Buddha learned from his disciple Ananda that the monks were expecting him to leave instructions when he died. They thought that if he left them rules and advice they would not feel so lonely and helpless without him. The Buddha had, however, only one answer.

The death of the Buddha

Think spot

Look at the story of the raft again. It will give you some idea how Buddha replied to Ananda's story about the instructions.

When you have thought about it write down your idea of the answer the Buddha gave. Then read on.

The Buddha told Ananda that the Sangha should depend on themselves, rely on the Dharma (his teaching) and not on anyone or anything else. All the monks in the Sangha were equal. Although they were expected to respect each other, there could be no leader. Only the Dharma could give them the answers to any questions that they might have.

About three months after this discussion the Buddha grew very tired. He asked for a couch and told his monks to bring in the local people. The monks became very distressed for they knew that he was preparing for death. In the life history we have used for this book the poet tells us what the Buddha said.

The hour of parting is bound to come in the end. Now I have done what I could do for myself and for others. To stay here would be without any purpose.

Then we are told he went into four trances and after the fourth trance

He came face to face with everlasting peace.

The Buddha's followers were overwhelmed by the loss of their teacher but they did eventually carry out the funeral service. In India all bodies are burned and so it was that the Buddha's body was burned and his ashes collected. These were then divided up and sent to different places for safe-keeping. They were placed in memorials which are called *stupas*. You can see what stupas look like in the pictures.

Eventually many memorials and places of worship were created all over the world. The Buddha, of course, is not a god but his followers like to remember him and in this way are reminded of what they have to do to gain perfect peace.

The teachings of the Buddha live on. There are over 500 million people in the world who call themselves Buddhists. Some are monks and nuns but the majority are ordinary people. Those who try to follow the Eightfold Path do so through their everyday life. But even if you are not a Buddhist some of his teachings are still important enough for us to think about today.

Buddha in Lotus Flower

11
Your journey begins

Ever since the time of Buddha's enlightenment there have been men and women willing to give up everything to learn the meaning of the Four Noble Truths and to keep to the Eightfold Path. They are the Sangha, the community of Buddhist monks or *bhikkus*. Through them people can reach back to Buddha and his teaching. Their homes are the monasteries built and provided by others who follow Buddha but who have continued to live with their families and to be part of the general community.

Anyone who wishes to join the Sangha may enter the monastery for a trial period. Then if they or the abbot, who is the chief monk, think that they are right for the life of a monk or nun, the person may be ordained. This shows that there is a serious desire to be a monk and the other monks accept it. At the ceremony the new monk will receive a new name and a robe. He will have agreed to live by 227 rules in the *Vinaya* which will organise his life from that moment. Even so, although a monk has been ordained he may, if he wishes, leave the Sangha at any time.

The life the monks lead is very simple. Meditating, studying, working and attending ceremonies are all part of their daily experiences. They sleep for only short periods of time, have no money or possessions of their own, eat one meal a day and depend on the offerings of others for their daily food. In return they teach people about the Buddhist ideas and help in the communities in which their monasteries have been built or founded.

Just as you will find followers of Buddha across the world so you will find monks and monasteries. You do not have to come from a particular part of the world to be a monk. Buddhism is open to all and so you will find Buddhist temples in Germany, monasteries in Sussex, Chiswick and Western Scotland, and centres of Buddhism in America.

It seems that more and more people are becoming interested in the teachings of Buddha and it is from the Sangha that they can receive the help they need on the journey that they are about to make.

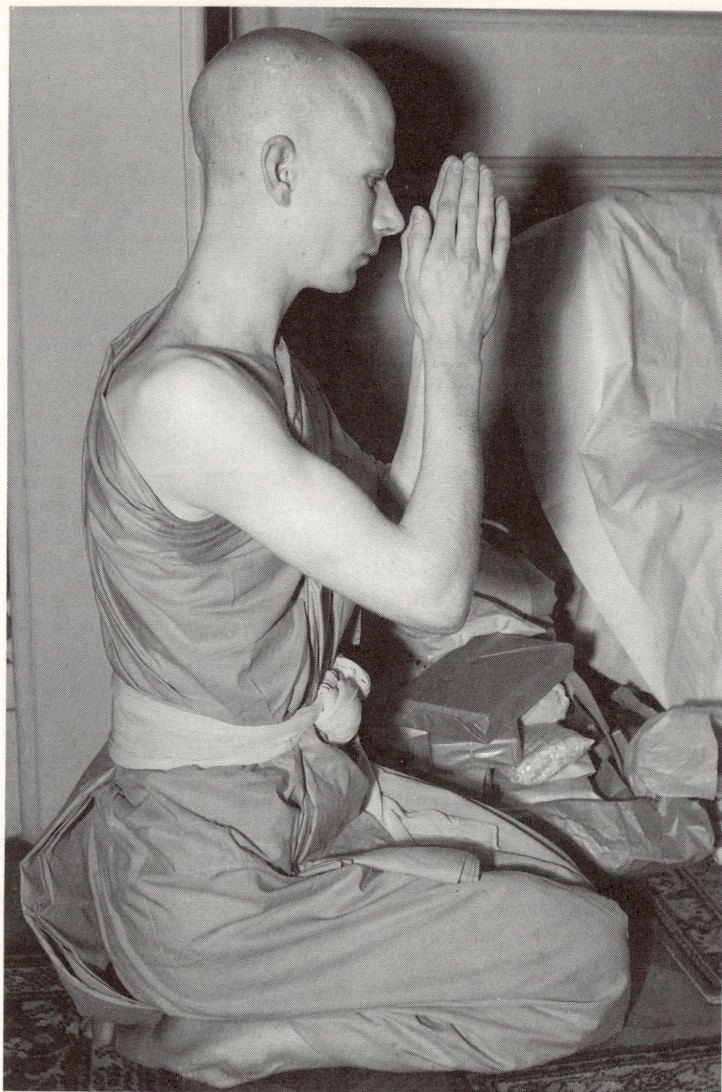

Think spot

Why do you think that there has been more interest in the life and teachings of Buddha during recent years?

It would be impossible to tell you everything about Buddhism itself in one book. This book's job was to help you to find out about Buddha and his teaching. Now the time has come for you to do some investigations of your own. We have listed some ideas for topics for you but of course you may have your own ideas about what you might like to do next.

1   How do Buddhist monks and nuns live and worship today?
2   What festivals are celebrated by the Buddhists? Find out the ceremonies and rituals that take place.
3   Find out how an ordinary person who is a Buddhist lives.
4   Read more stories about or told by the Buddha.
5   Collect pictures and pieces from newspapers that will show the meaning of the First and Second Noble Truths.
6   How do you think Buddhists feel about drug taking, animal experiments and nuclear weapons?
7   Write your own stories or poems that you think would help people to understand the Buddha's teachings.
8   Find as many pictures showing the Buddha as you can. In what ways are they different? In what ways are they the same? Give reasons for the differences and similarities.
9   Make or describe symbols or designs that will stand for some of the Buddha's ideas.
10 List the rules of a school that is trying to follow the Eightfold Path.

Glossary

This list of some important Buddhist terms will help you in your study. In this book the most common form is used. You may find some books use Pali (P) and others Sanskrit (S).

Word   **Meaning**

Anatta   'Not-self': the belief that a human being has no permanent 'soul' or 'self'.

Anicca   'Impermanence': the belief that all things, including human beings are constantly changing.

Bhikku   A member of the community of monks.

Bodhi   The name given to the tree beneath which Siddhartha attained enlightenment.

Buddha   'The enlightened one': a title which can be applied to any 'enlightened' person, this title usually refers to Siddhartha, the founder of Buddhism.

Dhamma (P) Dharma (S)   The whole body of the Buddha's teaching; 'the Truth' or 'perfect knowledge'.

Dukkha   Unsatisfactoriness: the belief that life inevitably involves sadness, loss, dissatisfaction, which can only be relieved by achieving enlightenment.

Gotama (P) Gautama (S)   The family name of the founder of Buddhism.

Kamma (P) Karma (S)   'Action': the belief that, for all beings, the quality of their thoughts and actions has an effect on what they become.

Nibbana (P) Nirvana (S)   The state of 'coolness' or 'perfect peace' which is realised when a person lets go of all self-interested attachments and desires. This state cannot be described, it can only be experienced.

Pali   The original language of Buddhist scriptures and discourse.

Pari-Nibbana (P) Pari-Nirvana (S)   The physical death of the Buddha; the final release from Samsara.

Samsara The cycle of existence, in which a person is bound until enlightenment is achieved.

Sangha The community of monks (and nuns).

Siddhatta (P) Siddhartha (S) The personal name of the founder of Buddhism.

Stupa A shrine, shaped like a bell, which helps Buddhists to remember the Buddha's teaching.

Tanha Craving, desire.

Vinaya The first part of the Scriptures containing the rules for the Sangha.

First published 1987

Published by
MACMILLAN EDUCATION LTD
Houndmills, Basingstoke, Hampshire RG21 2XS
and London
Companies and representatives
throughout the world

Printed in Hong Kong

British Library Cataloguing in Publication Data
Naylor, David,
Buddha: a journey. —— (Macmillan religious
studies in depth)
1. Buddha —— Biography   2. Buddhists ——
India —— Biography
I. Title   II. Smith, Ann, *1940*–
294.3'63   BQ882
ISBN 0–333–41595–7

ACKNOWLEDGEMENTS

The authors and publishers wish to thank Dawn Thompson for researching
the photographs, Peggy Morgan for advice on the text, Vera Lawrence for
preparing the manuscript, and the following for the use of copyright
material: James Clarke & Co Ltd for extracts from *One Man and His Dog* by
H. Lefevre, Lutterworth Press, 1973; and Penguin Books Ltd for extracts
from *Buddhist Scriptures* trans. by Edward Conze, Penguin Classics, 1959.
Copyright © Edward Conze, 1959.

The authors and publishers wish to acknowledge the following photo-
graph sources: Barclays Bank plc, p.30; BBC Enterprises, p.47; by kind permission of the Trustees of The British Museum, p.23; Camera Press, p.10
(top and bottom), 25 (centre right), 25 (bottom left); J. Allan Cash Ltd, pp. 9,
26 (bottom), 27; Douglas Dickins, p.48; FAO, p.25 (bottom right); John
and Penny Hubley, p.25 (top left); Lotus Cars Ltd, p.25 (centre left);
Mansell Collection, p.18; David Naylor, pp.21, 46; The Photo Source,
pp.15, 26 (top); Popperfoto, p.50; Staàtliches Museum für Völkerkunde,
cover; three cardinal faults illustration from *The World of Buddhism*, edited
by Heinz Bechert and Richard Gombrich, reproduced by kind permission
of Thames and Hudson Ltd, p.31;

The Publishers have made every effort to trace the copyright holders, but
where they have failed to do so they will be pleased to make the necessary
arrangements at the first opportunity.